Little People, BIG DREAMS™
GLORIA STEINEM

Written by
Maria Isabel Sánchez Vegara

Illustrated by
Lucila Perini

Frances Lincoln
Children's Books

Little Gloria came from Ohio, although she had always lived on the road with her parents and her older sister, Susanne. Wherever they went, their trailer was the Steinems' rolling home.

Gloria felt like she could do anything. She didn't see any difference between the friends that she made from place to place. No matter their gender, they could do the same things... or even better: they could do them together!

VINYLS

COMICS

Janis Joplin

SUPER HEROINE

She was ten when her parents divorced, and she settled with her mother in Toledo. For the first time in her life, Gloria attended school every day. But she soon realised that girls and boys were not treated the same there.

At that time, only boys were encouraged to study and get a good job, while girls were expected to get married and stay home with their children.

Even Gloria's mother had to give up her dream
of being a reporter, which made her feel terribly sad.

Her grandmother, Pauline, was a suffragist who had fought for equality and her granddaughters' right to vote. But when Gloria attended college, she never heard a word about the history of feminism or any other woman like her.

The day she first visited New York with her class, Gloria felt she had found her place. After two years studying in India, she went back to the city, ready to become a New Yorker and all that her mother had ever dreamt of: a journalist.

Soon, her witty and honest articles were everywhere! They challenged readers to see the world through Gloria's eyes. A world full of annoying rules against women, like losing the right to own a credit card once they were married.

To write some of her articles, Gloria had to go undercover. One time, she spent ten days dressed as a bunny to report on the working conditions that some women had to deal with. No one could even imagine there was a spy behind those ears!

Gloria had just interviewed John Lennon when she was asked to report on a meeting in a church basement organized by a feminist group. It was while listening to the speakers that she decided to join the women's liberation movement.

She soon realized there was a lot of work to do! Gloria helped start an organization that supported women in politics, as well as a groundbreaking female magazine that, within weeks, received more than 20,000 letters from readers!

For thirty years, she was one of the most popular voices of feminism, opening the door for fairer laws like the one that gave equal marriage rights.

She was 66 when David, an animal rights activist,
became her proud husband.

Together with her friend Jane Fonda, Gloria started the Women's Media Center which promotes equality through its amazing articles and stories. And she celebrated her 80th birthday by visiting elephants in Botswana.

And little Gloria will continue to inspire new generations of feminists ready to make the most out of their talents.

Because it doesn't matter what gender you are, what matters is that your dream is only yours to determine.

GLORIA STEINEM

(Born 1934)

c. 1944

1967

Gloria Marie Steinem was born on March 25th 1934 in Toledo, Ohio, USA. She spent her early years traveling with her family in a house trailer but settled after her parents divorced. At the age of ten, she took care of her mother, who was chronically depressed and constantly dismissed by doctors. This was the first time she witnessed anti-female bias. Gloria decided to study politics at college, a non-traditional choice for a woman at the time. After graduating in 1956, she went to India on a scholarship, where she participated in non-violent protests against government policy. She came back to the US and began working as a writer and journalist in New York City. By 1968, her work had become more political as her writing focused on progressive social issues, and she became more

1970

2021

involved with feminist groups. In 1971, Gloria co-founded *Ms.* magazine, a publication that was dedicated to championing women's rights, with African-American activist Dorothy Pitman Hughes. Gloria co-founded and formed other political feminist groups such as the National Women's Political Caucus, the Women's Action Alliance, and many more. In the 1990s, she helped establish Take Our Daughters to Work Day, the first national effort in the US to empower girls to learn more about their career opportunities. In 2013, President Barack Obama presented her with the Presidential Medal of Freedom for her work in the feminist movement. Through her grassroots feminism and powerful words, Gloria encourages a new generation of feminists to be the creators of their own dreams.

Want to find out more about **Gloria Steinem?**

Have a read of these great books:

Who is Gloria Steinem? (Who Was?) by Sarah Fabiny

Gloria Takes a Stand: How Gloria Steinem Listened, Wrote, and Changed the World by Jessica M. Rinker and Daria Peoples-Riley

Brimming with creative inspiration, how-to projects, and useful information to enrich your everyday life, Quarto Knows is a favourite destination for those pursuing their interests and passions. Visit our site and dig deeper with our books into your area of interest: Quarto Creates, Quarto Cooks, Quarto Homes, Quarto Lives, Quarto Drives, Quarto Explores, Quarto Gifts, or Quarto Kids.

Text © 2022 Maria Isabel Sánchez Vegara. Illustrations © 2022 Lucila Perini.
Original concept of the series by Maria Isabel Sánchez Vegara, published by Alba Editorial, SLU.
Little People Big Dreams and Pequeña&Grande are registered trademarks of Alba Editorial, SLU for books, publications and e-books. Produced under licence from Alba Editorial, SLU
First Published in the USA in 2021 by Frances Lincoln Children's Books, an imprint of The Quarto Group.
Quarto Boston North Shore, 100 Cummings Center, Suite 265D, Beverly, MA 01915, USA
Tel: +1 978-282-9590, Fax: +1 978-283-2742 **www.QuartoKnows.com**

ISBN 978-0-7112-7075-6
Set in Futura BT.
Published by Katie Cotton • Designed by Lyli Feng
Edited by Lucy Menzies • Production by Nikki Ingram
Editorial Assistance from Rachel Robinson
Manufactured in Guangdong, China CC112021
1 3 5 7 9 8 6 4 2

Photographic acknowledgements (pages 28-29, from left to right):

1. Gloria Steinem as a young girl in Michigan, Easter 1944 © Gloria Steinem Papers, Sophia Smith Collection, Smith College Special Collections 2. Feminist Gloria Steinem in a photograph, ca. 1967. © Bettmann via Getty Images 3. Writer and Critic Gloria Steinem, 1970 © Bettmann via Getty Images 4. NEW YORK, NEW YORK - JUNE 21: Feminist and activist Gloria Steinem speaks at a rally in support of mayoral candidate Maya Wiley the evening before the Democratic primary on June 21, 2021 in the Brooklyn borough of New York City. © Spencer Platt via Getty Images

Collect the *Little People,* **BIG DREAMS**™ series:

FRIDA KAHLO	COCO CHANEL	MAYA ANGELOU	AMELIA EARHART	AGATHA CHRISTIE	MARIE CURIE	ROSA PARKS	AUDREY HEPBURN

EMMELINE PANKHURST	ELLA FITZGERALD	ADA LOVELACE	JANE AUSTEN	GEORGIA O'KEEFFE	HARRIET TUBMAN	ANNE FRANK	MOTHER TERESA

JOSEPHINE BAKER	L. M. MONTGOMERY	JANE GOODALL	SIMONE DE BEAUVOIR	MUHAMMAD ALI	STEPHEN HAWKING	MARIA MONTESSORI	VIVIENNE WESTWOOD

MAHATMA GANDHI	DAVID BOWIE	WILMA RUDOLPH	DOLLY PARTON	BRUCE LEE	RUDOLF NUREYEV	ZAHA HADID	MARY SHELLEY

MARTIN LUTHER KING JR.	DAVID ATTENBOROUGH	ASTRID LINDGREN	EVONNE GOOLAGONG	BOB DYLAN	ALAN TURING	BILLIE JEAN KING	GRETA THUNBERG

JESSE OWENS	JEAN-MICHEL BASQUIAT	ARETHA FRANKLIN	CORAZON AQUINO	PELÉ	ERNEST SHACKLETON	STEVE JOBS	AYRTON SENNA

LOUISE BOURGEOIS	ELTON JOHN	JOHN LENNON	PRINCE	CHARLES DARWIN	CAPTAIN TOM MOORE	HANS CHRISTIAN ANDERSEN	STEVIE WONDER

MEGAN RAPINOE

MARY ANNING

MALALA YOUSAFZAI

ANDY WARHOL

RUPAUL

MICHELLE OBAMA

MINDY KALING

IRIS APFEL

ROSALIND FRANKLIN

RUTH BADER GINSBURG

MARILYN MONROE

KAMALA HARRIS

ALBERT EINSTEIN

CHARLES DICKENS

YOKO ONO

MICHAEL JORDAN

NELSON MANDELA

PABLO PICASSO

AMANDA GORMAN

GLORIA STEINEM

FLORENCE NIGHTINGALE

HARRY HOUDINI

J.R.R. TOLKIEN

ACTIVITY BOOKS

STICKER ACTIVITY BOOK

COLORING BOOK

LITTLE ME, BIG DREAMS JOURNAL

Discover more about the series at www.littlepeoplebigdreams.com